THE HOLISTIC ARTIST
An Exploration Into Art + Identity

Heath Hollensbe
Vernon Hyndman

ELYSIAN SOCIETY PRESS

The Holistic Artist
Copyright © 2018 by Heath Hollensbe and Vernon Hyndman

ISBN: 978-1-7321769-0-4
LCCN: 2018904528
First Edition

All rights reserved. No part of this book may be reproduced or transmitted in any form or by any means, electronic or mechanical, including photocopying, recording, or by an information storage and retrieval system - except by a reviewer who may quote brief passages in a review to be printed in a magazine or newspaper - without permission in writing from the publisher.

Contact the publisher by visiting www.ElysianSociety.com or by writing to Info@ElysianSociety.com.

Special Thanks to Dr. David McDonald (http://doctordavidmcdonald.com/). God accidentally forgot to turn off the spigot of creativity and intelligence as He was filling up David's brain.

Like a nice scotch... Sip this book slowly. Too much at one sitting is wasteful.

Printed in the United States Of America

DEDICATION

This book is for all the creatives out there who used to feel passionate and gifted, and hopeful that they could change the world, but who have since lost that energy or had it beaten out of them.

And for the artists who have been silenced because they were not understood, or improperly misunderstood. This book is a meager offering of how we are fighting to give you hope again… And a promise that we will continue to, until we take our last breath.

CONTENTS

1. **Rocket-Ships And Roller-Skates**
2. **Replication Is Regurgitation**
3. **The Destination Is Not The End Point**
4. **Complexity Is Not Usually Better**
5. **Art Does Not Need To Be Preachy**
6. **Separate Art From Self-Expression**
7. **No Agenda**
8. **Your Art Should Always Be Open To Being Modified**
9. **Excellence Is A Horrible Dictator**
10. **Expectations Will Smother You To Death**
11. **Good Art Does Not Believe In Atheists**
12. **Disorder The Orderly (But Leave The Nurse Alone)**
13. **Stimulate Yourself, Then Others**
14. **Busyness Suffocates The Soul**
15. **Disregard Any Suggestion Of The Sacred/Secular Divide**
16. **Do Not Be A POV Bully**
17. **Culture...Schmulture**
18. **Editing Will Castrate Your Work**
19. **Create. Stop. Present. Stop. Repeat.**
20. **Create Art That Someone Would Rescue From Your Casket**

21	**No One Likes The Hall Monitor**
22	**IDEAlism**
23	**Leave The Tradition At Nana's House**
24	**Art Needs The Best Of You**
25	**Make Art, Not Anesthesia**
26	**Prejudice Pursues You**
27	**Art As A Colonic**
28	**Comfort is Overrated**
29	**Chaos Is Necessary, Irrationality Is A Rational Approach**
30	**Imagine No Resistance**
31	**Home Is Not Where The heART Is**
32	**Self-Doubt 101**
33	**What Does Freedom Feel Like?**
34	**Hatred And All Things Evil**
35	**Profit vs. Prophet**
36	**Incoherence Is Not A Virtue**
37	**Do Not Resign Too Quickly**
38	**Ahoy There!**
39	**Addiction Is Overrated**
40	**Love Yourself, But Do Not Gloat**

INTRODUCTION

Art: the various branches of creative activity
Identity: the fact of being who or what a person or thing is

This book was originally created as a "40 Days Of Lent" experience of what artists need to die to. As with any breathing organism, things took a shape of their own, so we jumped into the river to see where this project would lead us.

We are quite proud of where this landed, but we are the dads in this case. We hope you enjoy consuming as much as we enjoyed writing.

When we started this crucifixion of bad ideas, we became convinced that some of the worst offenders, most deserving of being nailed to the cross, actually escaped out the back door.

What started as a straightforward crucifixion of art enemies morphed into a bit of a rave, a sort of artistic kegger… and in this mid-writing change, we demonstrate in our art what we are trying to articulate with our words… the damn thing just did what it wanted, and we were along for the ride. Fasten your seatbelt. Hold my beer.

We would be honored if you disagree with what we have to say occasionally. We would be most proud if some of the comments that you are about to read frustrate you and make you angry and grab your attention by the throat. By the way, the cover of this book makes an excellent dartboard, which might be a useful means of coming to terms with the parts that stick in your craw.

Take your time. Mentally wrestle these ideas to the mat. Steal them. Make them yours. Rip a page out and tape it to your mirror. Use whatever we offer to find life and art.

Oh, and then get off your ass and go make something.

We are already proud of you.

CONCEPT 001
/// Rocket-Ships And Roller-Skates ///

You have been unfairly over-praised and over-appreciated.

Art does not grow in the garden of praise. Stop allowing other's over-gushing of you to keep you from pressing harder to discover yourself. Do not settle for unwarranted compliments. You are far too complex for that.

Refuse to be a clone of what you have been, what someone else has been; refuse to be the outcome of what someone else wants you to be. Do not replicate, originate.

You were created to be a rocket-ship; you will die unhappy and unfulfilled if you settle to be a pair of roller-skates.

Many artists are satisfied with copying what they have seen previously because they are unsure of their true identity.

If you are not deliberately true to your identity, praise or criticism will disillusion you. It will allow you to bend and compromise who you are to please the people that are voicing opinions that are not really that important to you in the first place. As a result, you will render your art to this disillusionment rather than to a fresh expression of who you really are.

Mine deep into who you really are and die to what everyone else wants you to be.

Understand your unique shape.

Know who you are not.

CONCEPT 002
/// Replication Is Regurgitation ///

Formulas provide a beautiful framework for existence, but the role of an artist is to see the world with fresh eyes. Artists turn inside out what the world has accepted as reality.

Familiarity with formula, particularly one that has brought pleasure to you in the past, is the greatest temptation to replicate your own previous creativity. Replication is regurgitation… even if you are replicating yourself.

The trap of previous success becomes the hamster-wheel of an assembly-line artist. The problem with assembly line artists is that they are often forgotten. Don't create to be forgotten.

Acknowledge the formula, tip your hat to what was and move on.

A good artist is a master at smashing things that do not belong together, rendering something new and beautiful. Be a master smasher!

Understand the formulas so that you are aware of what to break. Study formulas and become acquainted with them, but treat formulas like a ditch to be avoided. Have a broad enough understanding of them so that you can forget about them and spend your art working past them.

Never trust a formula, for it was created for some previous time, and for some previous artist. You see this often in church music (verse, chorus, verse, chorus, bridge, chorus, chorus) or in a pastor's 3-point sermon notes.

Do not respect formulas or give your energy to loving or hating them. Let unoriginality be. Leave formulas in the museum of previous art.

Formulas are meant to be toyed with, and your job as an artist is to ensure that happens.

CONCEPT 003
/// The Destination Is Not The End Point ///

Our lives beg us to move from one thing to the next, aimlessly wandering towards our expiration date. Sadly, (perhaps as a coping mechanism) we invest imagination into a version of ourselves that we hope to experience in 20 years rather than being invested in our own presence today.

Stop dreaming of who you will be in two decades and start producing with who you are today.

We are tempted to not complete projects because our perception of the work does not fit with our perfect vision of what should be. We disqualify ourselves because the art we create today does not perfectly fit in with our imagined perfect future self. In fact, almost every project that I have ever worked on fits into this category. I get so paralyzed with the end product that I do not enjoy the process at all.

The answer to the creative challenge rests in a holistic understanding of your identity.

Great art will be produced the more you invest in your true identity at this moment, rather than some future possibility.

Inspiration is banging around inside of you, begging to be released. Do not procrastinate. Do not trade this moment for some moment in the future. Use the inspiration that is inside you begging for freedom and beat your reality into something beautiful.

Breathe.

Let the moment, and your inspiration, and your energy explode into art and refuse to miss even one heartbeat. Live in the here and now and embrace everything that life is throwing at you.

Follow the road, see where it leads. Don't fall victim to the lie that you are making the road, or that you have to know where you are going.

CONCEPT 004
/// Complexity Is Not Usually Better ///

Art makes a clear statement in a noisy complex world.

If you are anything like me, many of your pieces have never seen the light of day because they get dissolved in a labyrinth of rabbit trails; my artistic message is often lost in the dilution of competing for other messages, that in the creative process, all suddenly seem important. As a result, I tend to not produce anything and end up scrapping the project altogether.

Over-communication is the arch-enemy of mystery. We complicate things unnecessarily. The reason that we make things complex is because we are unsatisfied with our simple offerings and we are afraid that others would share in that dissatisfaction.

Elegant beats busy. Simple appeals to the senses more effectively than the complex. Do not attempt to reproduce the complete Library of Congress in one artistic act; work from what you are drawn to.

Work towards what you find beautiful.

Simple is beautiful, but believe it or not, making simple art is much harder to do than making complex art. Why? Because simplicity is a nugget that requires that you work harder and better to refine your creative product. An artist is an expert butcher, cutting off the fat while producing lean, high-quality red meat. Simplify to the simplest point, then make it simpler.

Die to the impulse that you need to overstate and over communicate.

Become proficient at minimizing.

CONCEPT 005
/// Art Does Not Need To Be Preachy ///

Frank Schaeffer wrote a great book called "Addicted to Mediocrity," in which he criticized Christian art for being flaccid, uninspiring, and derivative.

You are an amazing creation, embrace the creative DNA that was breathed into the dust that makes you.

Your artistry does not define you. You are far more fascinating than what you produce. Artistry is not your identity; artistry emanates from your identity.

Everyone living out of their True (God-given) identity is an artist. Because of that, you should feel the freedom to put something of yourself in your art.

Start to get comfortable with the person that inhabits your skin. There is no wrong art, only cheesy false identities.

All of your art will in some way, communicate "gospel" concepts such as freedom and love because the reflection of your own identity that you invest in your art has the image of God.

Please don't boil art down to a pathetic version of a blonde hair/blue-eyed white Jesus in a garden. Look deeper. Good art is not a caricature of Jesus, as great as caricatures are. Not every portrait has to be of Jesus, because even Jesus did not incessantly talk about himself all the time.

If all truth is God's truth (Hint: it is), then be free to create true art because God is in all that is true.

CONCEPT 006
/// Separate Art From Self-Expression ///

Art was always meant to provide a place of common ground for people. To unify people in truth. To work against the natural instinct to do things apart from one another. The best artists find common ground like a beachhead and invite people to share common ground.

Self-expression is not art. Self-expression is like a little child who throws tantrums at a museum. Cute? More annoying than cute. Able to change the world? Not a chance.

Put yourself into your art, but not at the expense of it.

Art invites people into a world that is bigger than self, bigger than local community, bigger than the concepts and ideas that you feel comfortable with and have been taught since you were a child.

By confusing art with self-expression, you end up creating reflective art next to the pool with Narcissus - vomiting reflective self - expression as if every piece were a self-portrait, hijacking the beauty of true art.

Art invites people into the eternal stream of humanity. You are a shore fisherman of the abstract and so go fishing to feed your whole tribe. Avoid fishing in chlorinated pools, even though they are comfortable and predictable.

CONCEPT 007
/// No Agenda ///

There is a new god in town: Deus Obvious. That's right. Our culture wants everything to be explained, easy-to-comprehend, and immediately available for application.

And no one worships Deus Obvious with more fervor than pastors.

As a result, "church art" has all the subtly of a crotch-kick.

Art (in the worship of money) demands that the artist trade identity and calling. Money worship is the prostitution of art, whoring creativity out for a quick sale.

Sex without commitment is art without a soul. Prostituted art becomes bland, sterile and dumbed down to appease the lowest common denominator of purchaser. No one wants to be remembered as the person who sells their body for a quick buck, why do the same with your art?

Good art does not need to be explained or qualified.

Explaining art is like explaining jokes - Something is lost in the process.

Art evokes meaning in the person who is experiencing the art, awakening something that is already there inside the human experience. No need to be coddled, inexplicable art resolves in the continued experience of the audience.

Don't be the comedian who has to explain each joke.

CONCEPT 008
/// Your Art Should Always Be Open To Being Modified ///

Good art is iterative and living. Engage the energy, ideas, and suggestions of others. Your identity is secure if others contribute. Your next breath is on loan from God, all truth you discover is His genius, and your art is stealing from the existence that He has already created. So, there is no need to be possessive or defensive.

Release your art. Good art is secure in its identity and purpose and is not insecure about taking on the suggestions and modifications by others. Maybe the art that you create will be enhanced in 500 years by another artist with a technology that is yet to be imagined.

Do not fall into the trap that you are the sole author of the piece and when you decide that it is done, that it is finished.

Good art breathes and lives on forever.

Creating art that you demand must be finished is essentially adding an epitaph to your piece. No one determines what their death will look like; they see where life leads them, and death is the end of it. You should view your art the same way. Do not create with the end in mind. While epitaphs are respectful, they mark the dead -

and the dead are always soon forgotten. Make living art that demands a dance with new technology and new mediums. Invest in artists yet to be born.

Good art should always be open to being adapted and modified as it will always allow for the expansion of other people's ideas. Good art is a raft floating down the eternal river of humanity. New mediums and subsequent artists reinterpret and reinvigorate art.

Radzimir Dębski is creatively remixing hip-hop music into orchestra scores. David Irvine paints random pop-culture characters into iconic portraits. Ultimately, these artists are re-working art that has been beautifully produced in the first place… and in doing so, they are breathing fresh air onto the piece again.

Art can (and should) be modified and changed and added to, without it being reduced. Dead art stops adapting and maturing, and once that happens, it is ready for the trashcan. (Do not even get me started on copyrights and intellectual property.)

Time works against static art.

CONCEPT 009
/// Excellence Is A Horrible Dictator ///

How heartbreaking is it to hear of an artist who fails to create for fear the product will be less than the dream? Where does this destructive idea originate? How tragic that so many great pieces never end up seeing the light of day because a creator does not believe the art is "good enough" yet.

Perfectionism is an illusion, and it is one of the primary reasons that artists are being handicapped in their calling.

What qualifies as perfect, anyway? A good artist is constantly changing, adapting, maturing and evolving, and will continue to do that until the day that they die.

Perfectionism is pre-failing by design.

Even if you are perfectly happy with the project that you are working on, one day you will look back on it and see that you don't hold it as "perfect" as it was when it was created (I will do the same with this book). Let your art move and adapt with you as you progress through life. Let yourself be all the ages.

Create and release stuff. Be unapologetic with your work. Then grow up and create new stuff.

Let the imperfections join the show!

Do not allow the undertaker to bury your art with you.

CONCEPT 010
/// Expectations Will Smother You To Death ///

A good artist needs to be free from unrealistic expectations.

"Expectation" is energy given to outcomes before outcomes are played out. Many people never get started because the expectations they place upon themselves crush them before they are free to dream. If you are letting other people's expectations of you dictate what you create, then you are not an artist. You are giving up your seat as an artist to them. You move from artist to the nerdy kid hanging around the cool kids, begging to be liked.

Expectations are a terrible and relentless dictator that will never allow you to be confident in what you are creating. Much like perfectionism, expectations are a terrible illusion.

Build a limit to the expectations of others, and be careful of your own expectations. Living with your art in the moment means giving all of your energy to the present, and expectations are for some imagined future.

Do not allow unrealistic expectations to define who you are and what you create. Do not serve that prison time.

Create out of passion and identity rather than what other people are expecting. Expectations are handcuffs to which you hold the key. Unlock them. Expectations have no power over you that you do not expressly allow.

Refuse to be a creative that is shackled by the made-up false expectations of your imagination.

False expectations are a debilitating monster under the bed; producing fear, but susceptible to the light of truth. False expectations create an impenetrable fake wall that seems impossible to overcome. Expectations steal all the joy that is found in actually creating something worthwhile.

After all, expectations are premeditated resentments.

CONCEPT 011
/// Good Art Does Not Believe In Atheists ///

Never trust a creative who denies anything categorically. You may as well ask a horse with blinders for a peripheral glance.

Art is designed to frustrate our perceptions and disillusion our reality-grounding constructs. By limiting our ideas of what is possible based off of what has been quantifiably proven, we eliminate the potential of an entire realm of possibility. Even the most committed denier might self-avail an opportunity to mock the imaginary; absolute denial precludes great satire.

An artist who denies some form of existence (based on what they have experienced) is creating art with an agenda - properly called propaganda. Do not trust propaganda. Denial is not merely a river in Africa; the art of a denier is as dangerous as single ply toilet paper.

Disbelieving takes far too much energy away from art.

Agenda subjugates art because art needs the vulnerability of possibility to thrive. This is not to say that art does not fight for itself, but art should not have to fight its own birth-artist.

A cosmos of possibility is fertilized soil to great creativity. The power of metaphor is lost with impulse to explain. Anti-religious art rivals tawdry religious art for insignificance.

If you are going to be defiant, at least embrace what you will mock. At least a Judas kiss allows the viewer the fiction that your message is somewhat nuanced propaganda.

CONCEPT 012
/// Disorder The Orderly (But Leave The Nurse Alone) ///

Bowing down to rigid order is the enemy of the creative mind. In fact, it is a prison cell to freedom-loving art.

Order is a demand of the audience, not the freedom cry of the artist. Ordered art meets expectations, yet where is the art in expectations? Humans hack order out of a random universe and lose their wonder in the predictability of their self-ordered world. Order is the hated hall monitor, appeasing adult expectations while crushing the wild abandon of childhood.

Let your breakup with order be amicable, yet final.

Recently, a date night for my wife and I was a progressive dinner around our city with some of our closest friends. The evening was so organized that it felt constrained like a too-tight polyester suit. Our group eventually ditched the regiment for few bottles of good wine. We sat on a rooftop milling about in contented disorganization. We literally took off the neckties constricting our airways. We were free, free to be our casual selves, resulting in a date night that we will remember forever.

Disorder provides its own rewards.

From disorder comes randomness and from randomness comes possibility.

Disorder frees your art from the constraints of your limited imagination, transitioning you from the center stage of your art to a front row seat of your own creative process.

CONCEPT 013
/// Stimulate Yourself, Then Others ///

Is loneliness the enemy or breeding ground for your creativity? God acknowledged Adam's loneliness, with a hat tip to his own desire for community with Adam.

Relational stimulation inspires, perseveres, creates, appreciates, affirms. The first artistic pursuit recorded; man and woman, in symbiotic relationship, naming the animals. After they named the fly, oh to be the fly on the wall, observing them argue, laugh, bitch & moan, and lose themselves in makeup sex.

The creative process requires times of solitude to process, create and wrestle.

In fact, Cormac McCarthy is such a hilarious recluse that his own agent has never met him!

However, isolation does not allow the grit of community to sand art down to be everything that it could be.

Others are so much more intelligent than we are and see things more beautifully that we do. Are willing to ask deeper and better questions that expose us to greater thought?

Community offers varied gifts; intelligence, creativity, inquisitive nature… what arrogance to think that we can create alone better than in community.

There will be times when solitude and being alone are the greatest balm possible for our weary minds and hearts, but solitude is best in small doses.

CONCEPT 014
/// Busyness Suffocates The Soul ///

Each of us have 525,600 minutes a year (I eternally bow at your genius, Jonathan Larson[1]). Why are some able to accomplish so much in a year while others slip through an accomplishment-free year? Is it about our capacity? Does it have more to do with our schedules slowly eating away at the time that is needed to reflect and dream?

If creativity is encoded in our DNA, why are we so willing to let the mundane eat away at the time that we were given to dream and create?

Steven Pressfield calls procrastination the enemy of art. I would clarify that busyness is the mortal enemy of art, though I would gladly admit that I believe procrastination and busyness to be two sides of the same coin.

If your life is running from here to there without any payoff or passion, then you are allowing your frantic business to suffocate your creative soul.

Busyness is a silent killer, not taken seriously enough until too late.

---

[1] Larson is the brilliant mind behind many broadway shows including Rent (My personal favorite). Larson died unexpectedly the morning of *Rent*'s first preview performance Off Broadway and never got to see his show hit the stage. However, I would encourage you to download "Seasons Of Love" and then sit back and enjoy an audio orgasm.

You know for years leading up to it that you should take better precautions on how to deal with it, but before you know it... we fight a sneaking suspicion that time is slipping by, until the day you are in a refrigerator with a tag on your toe and nothing to show for your life.

Fight for your schedule.

Fight for your time.

Declutter.

Be aggressive in cutting the things out of your iCal that are not going to produce artistic fruit.

Every day spends 115,200 heartbeats that you are never going to get back. Fight to make each one of those heartbeats count!

CONCEPT 015
/// Disregard Any Suggestion Of The Sacred-Secular Divide ///

Art is the expression of the entire being, body, soul, and spirit, sustaining the world. Throw your whole being into what you create.

Your thoughts…

Your emotions…

Your convictions…

Everything.

There is no moderation in commitment. The world is more than willing to control you and your art.

Not long ago, I was driving in Texas (God bless the Bible Belt) and came across a building that had "Christian Office Supplies" on it. They were a company that created just that - Christian office supplies. What in the literal hell does that mean? Honestly? Have the staplers been washed in the blood of the Lamb? Are the 3-hole-punches filled with the Spirit of God more than the ones that you would buy at Office Depot?

Do not be so foolish to think that God shops at Lifeway Christian stores and only listens to positive and encouraging radio.

He can handle reality.

Do not buy the religious lie to only engage whatever is presented as "Christian."

God created one world and called it blessed.

He still loves the world and is actively involved in the affairs of the world.

So, for Christ's sake (literally), let's stop dividing the world that He created.

CONCEPT 016
/// Do Not Be A POV Bully ///

Everyone deserves to have a voice – an aspect of human rights (of which I am a huge proponent). Exercise the discipline of receiving input and consideration from anyone.

What are you creating that sticks out as a megaphone among all the other chatter? Being a megaphone is less about screaming to share your voice and so much more about gaining the respect needed to cut through all the other mediocrity.

Maintain your own point of view. Know why you believe what you believe. Be ready to share why you believe what you do and why you are fighting for what you are fighting for.

Your point of view is grounded in your subjective reality (place, time, circumstance and history). Beyond your subjective reality, what is it that you are trying to communicate that is timeless?

Your art is a time traveler to the future, the present and the past. It needs to be able to transcend time and location, and preference and culture.

Your art should look other-worldly.

Don't believe me? Look at amazing pieces of art (Beethoven is a great example, 200 years later) that seem to always be pertinent and adaptable to current society.

Create art that studies and incorporates culture. The secret sauce is found in the adaptation and innovation of the eternal.

CONCEPT 017
/// Culture... Schmulture ///

Always borrow from culture, but don't be culture's bitch... Consider culture and incorporate wisdom to address cultural reality and modify to shift culture's lens.

Culture reveals the heart and the needs of people who are trying to make sense of life. It is important to study culture and then offer an alternative lens on how to see things.

I have been surrounded by people who ignore culture because they are not willing to consider what culture appreciates (mostly because they believe that it has to be Biblical "truth").

Should an artist be able to enter into the deepest darkness and try to make sense of it? The answer is yes!

To be the best artist, you must be willing to enter the discomfort.

Be willing to shoulder the doubt of others. That is where the search for truth begins.

Be cautious of the folks that try to tame and minimize you! Do not allow others to stifle creativity. Do not reduce the mysteries of doubt and hurt by logic. Do not trust them. Enter into the hurt and confusion and get comfortable.

Let art make sense of it and then flow through you. It is only then that your creativity will strive.

CONCEPT 018
/// Editing Will Castrate Your Work ///

We all have an internal editor. Create, but only after you duct tape your internal editor to a chair in the next room.

The second-guessing of what you are creating will stop you from producing the beautiful art that is resonating in your soul.

Hire an editor later in the process to provide feedback. Paid editors have a very specific job, as do you! There is an editor everywhere, but artists are rare. Lock the editor out until the piece is complete. As an artist, it is important to know your value in the world.

Avoid the oversimplification that editors are left brained - and artists are right brained. We are one body and many parts. Do not to get so lost in the weeds of correction that you fail to produce the very thing that is resonating in your soul.

A great artistic tragedy I have witnessed is the self-editing, yet non-producing artist attempting to both create and edit at the same time.

Free yourself to run freely with the art you are producing and trust that editors will be ready when you need them.

Resist creating and editing simultaneously.

There will be plenty of time later to spell correctly and to place a comma.

CONCEPT 019
/// Create. Stop. Present. Stop. Repeat. ///

What is art without tension? Movie directors and movie critics. Michelin star chefs and professional critics of their work. Artists and observers. Fans and cynics.

Sadly, many artists miss their calling as they grasp for some false method – they get so excited about being an artist that they attempt shit that they are terrible at.

Imagine Bono taking the stage, setting up an art easel and silently painting modified stick figures for two hours?

Or Tom Cruise starting a jazz band.

It just does not work.

Good art needs no sales. Observers are captured, grasped by the shoulders; art whispers to its audience, "You need me in your life!" Art seeks out its audience, not the other way around.

Art is not desperate, not insecure; art leaves that for the artist to wrestle with. Art does not lose sleep or question its purpose. Art is still art, regardless of reception.

Create for art's sake, your being, and your perspective coming out in the medium. Be the passionate artist who is present for creation. Do not let the self-editing narrator in your head guide your art. Do not give in to the instinct to present and narrate your art, to explain your art; stop what you are doing, take a few steps back and then breathe.

Do not confuse mystery with unintelligibility; the profound and the idiotic both cause wonder, but the idiotic leaves a bad taste.

Art requires us to ponder, to wonder, and to imagine.

Open-minded audiences will search for meaning in art, and will remain searching until some meaning manifests; pray that they do not arrive at, "Aha, I have it, the artist is an idiot."

Do not preach, do not explain, just be true to yourself and your art. Preachy art is shoved into the audience's face belligerently. Showcase art - do not shove it. Attraction, not promotion.

Offer the best of your identity. The most reliable way to come across desperate and annoying is to try to be like someone else.

CONCEPT 020
/// Create Art That Someone Would Rescue From Your Casket ///

For years, I traveled with different famous bands around the world. On one particular occasion, the group that I traveled with met in my room at a hotel for community including nightcaps and laughter. Noticing the wall art, one of my friends commented that they had the same exact piece of art hanging over the bed in their room. Others chimed in, and we realized that the same picture was in every room.

Artists want to create desire, but not to be mass produced.

While replication might make more money, there is a dilution that artists avoid. The pragmatic art industry allows businessmen to use artists to exploit art for a quick buck.

Unoriginal art is like getting junk mail. The worst that can be said about an artist; the audience regrets their investment.

When an audience finds great art, no one has to explain why the art is good; great art is self-evident.

The best art initiates desire. Its value is partly in how little great art is available.

You will be in a box soon enough, and others will have all you have created.

Make art that people want to steal.

CONCEPT 021
/// No One Likes The Hall Monitor ///

Nazis, afraid of the power of art, organized book burnings and declared art they disagreed with "degenerate art." No higher praise, in my opinion, could be awarded art than to be labeled degenerate by a Nazi.

Resist the urge to fix the world.

Resist the urge to sanitize.

Unfortunately, art cannot sanitize the world, it can only sanitize, and therefore, neuter itself.

There are very few things that I can think of that I hate more than being in the presence of people who are constantly keeping moral score. The job of a hall monitor must be exhausting, with the judgement meter pegged to the max all the time. My bet is the person who likes the hall monitor least is the hall monitor; judgement is projected self-loathing.

Moralism makes bad art. Moralism is "should-ing" on people; moralism refuses to accept people as they are and constantly demands that people be as we think they should.

Moralistic art is propaganda with a judgmental message, an artistic form of self-hatred. Moralists pride themselves on self-described moral superiority, which reveals hatred for their own humanity.

Love people as they are, love yourself as you are, and it is in this pure love of humanity that non-toxic improvement grows. Self-acceptance is not an excuse for imperfection except in the courtroom of a moralistic judge. Self-acceptance inherently hopes for improvement through love.

Be honest in your art. Let the world be what it is and represent what it is with your art.

Even assholes serve a purpose in this world; who better to increase appreciation for the grace of the humble?

Moralistic art is a feeble attempt in polishing turds. However, in the end, shiny turds are still turds.

Let the world be what it is, and comment on what you see.

CONCEPT 022
/// IDEAlism ///

Art can be like the changing-room of an expensive clothier; a place where people who can't afford the clothes can still try them on.

It is one thing to see Nirvana and express the desire that other-worldliness evokes, and quite another to move to Nirvana and send your art home. Beware of becoming disconnected from the lives around you. A head full of existentialism is cute and exciting for a while, but audiences tire of art that does not meet real life.

Leave enough room for the lives and interpretations of others.

Resist the urge to demand that your own interpretation be the "right" one.

People see art as they are, and as they hope to be, or as they desperately hope not to be, not as art is. Leave space in your art.

Let art be enough, do not drag people around to the points you are forcing on them. Invite them into your reality to poke around and discover what they will. Most folks will at least notice your point.

Be secure enough to allow people their own interpretation. Give people permission to allow their minds to be curious, to explore, to break out of their day-to-day preconceptions. To lead people into places of thought by re-shifting their minds is a high calling of art.

Invite people to explore, don't shame them for their lack of freedom.

Show them why it is beautiful.

Show them what could be.

Find beauty in the mud.

Find art on the edges of life, the vast majority of people never venture out from the center.

CONCEPT 023
/// Leave The Tradition At Nana's House ///

Familiarity breeds contempt. I have always loved that line.

The risk-taking side of me is quenched when I am tempted to abide by tradition. A reactive instinct in me demands that I de-sanctify traditions. What is this evil? I truly enjoy watching the squirm of those who hold the "but-we've-always-done-it-this-way" banner? What I know is that whether I detest tradition, or embrace tradition, either way, tradition has my focus.

What if tradition were the diving board we use to launch us into the pool of possibility?

The draw to tradition and repetition is an energy sink to someone whose mind is wired like a bloodhound to sniff out new and fresh and edgy.

Tradition is the reliable brake pedal for artists, which believes the fear that audiences and artists share of being challenged out of circles of comfort. *"What has always been"* is such an easy scapegoat.

The denial of tradition is like a parent-hating teen.

Traditional in small doses invoke stories that guide and facilitate art. A little salt on a meal is heaven, but just a little. The meal is not about salt, and so art cannot be about tradition.

Challenge tradition.

Use it.

Modify it.

Redeem it.

Just don't idolize it.

CONCEPT 024
/// Art Needs The Best Of You ///

Artists often create and innovate out of frustration, hurt and anger. Renegades seek to remediate their past by pouring all their frustrations into their hoping for change.

Anger makes an attractive daydream - more of a cute illusion than a practical solution.

It is the 5-year-old fantasizing about kicking the bad guy in the nuts.

Cute? Absolutely… Practical? Not a chance in hell.

Artists give their work a voice.

Let difficulty and frustration be fertile soil for your art to grow. Plant seeds of frustration and reap a crop of crappy art.

Be the ground in which beauty grows.

Neediness produces desperate art.

Woe to the artist whose motive is applause. Wounded people make art about their needs.

Art reveals the best part of you showcasing your perspective, wounds will have you fighting with your audience for attention.

Give art your strength, not your need.

CONCEPT 025
/// Make Art, Not Anesthesia ///

Exploring pain is one of the greatest motivating factors in the production of great art. Why? Because artists are willing to go there. Willing to rehash what they have experienced and face it head-on.

It is absolutely necessary to embrace the dark aspects of life. Invite your most hurtful memories to dinner and ask them to share their story. Listen attentively and compassionately. Enter into the story. Let the story overtake you.

Pain is a beautiful catalyst for honest art.

It would be a shame if you attempt to neuter your art by numbing the pain. Exploring pain is very different from giving art your need. Pain and need are indicators on the dashboard of life, though they do not directly move the car. Pay attention to the indicators on your dashboard, but do not allow pain and need to drive the car. Denied pain is no guarantee that pain will not show up in the very things that you create.

Do not be so quick to call for anesthetic.

Numbing blunts the very parts of your brain that will ultimately respond to difficulty. Do not become numb to or distracted from the reality of what has/is happening to you.

Sit with the pain.

Breathe in the hurt.

Do not rationalize or minimize the pain that you are feeling. It is really there and is absolutely valid.

Stare it in the face. Then, leave pain in its cage and go create what you have just experienced.

CONCEPT 026
/// Prejudice Pursues You ///

The artistic process can become contaminated with prejudice.

Art is particularly susceptible at the beginning of a project to prejudice in the sneaky way of presuming what the piece is going to be. Prejudging artistic work can railroad art and miss the best possibility. Hold the concept loosely and let it be birthed from your being, not ripped out by the roots.

Imagine telling a child in a womb that they are going to be a paleontologist at the age of 27. Such presuming shackles, confines and improperly forces your will on what the piece could actually become. Prejudging removes any trust and dependence on energy and creative moments to break into your world.

Art is a living and breathing progeny that invites us through a variety of setbacks, switchbacks and redefining, reassessing and correcting.

To prejudge from the onset is ultimately signing its death certificate before the project even has legs to walk. Let art take a breath and think. Let the recurring impulse catch you off guard. Do not destroy the life of your piece before you ever birth it.

Stop profiling your art. Admit you have no clue where it comes from or where it is going. Walk with your art and enjoy the company.

Let art end up where is going to end up. Stop proving and presuming... It confines and imprisons something that has so much more potential when you do not throw your prerogative at it.

CONCEPT 027
/// Art As A Colonic ///

The brain and the sphincter were discussing which part of the body is most important... the brain waxed eloquent about poetry, and calculus, and the poetry of calculus... the hand pointed to art and work because pointing is one of the hand's best capabilities. The hand also mentioned to the entire body that food intake is dependent on it. The applause was deafening, and it appeared the hand would be proven the most important body part. The sphincter was strangely quiet, and the quiet continued. Everyone wondered what it would say, yet the sphincter said nothing. The sphincter just clammed up, literally. None shall pass. Nothing. And before long, the brain fogged up, and the hands wrung, and everyone prevailed upon the sphincter to open, to release, to do what sphincters do, yet it refused. Unanimously, the body voted that the sphincter truly is the most important part of the body... and the sphincter relaxed and again did what sphincters do.

Culture has a way of eating itself into a constipation that fogs the brain over. No fiber and before long, there is a brick to be dealt with, sideways.

Sometimes art can be the rectal suppository, the laxative, the colonic that loosens the grip and solves the problem.

Sometimes the asshole is the most important.

Depends on what you need.

CONCEPT 028
/// Comfort Is Overrated ///

If you have ever spent a day at the beach, listening hypnotically to the waves as they land, you have experienced the sinusoid of life in a visceral way. In and out. We have highs and lows. Ups and downs. Wins and losses. Just when we're feeling at home with a disappointment, the world starts working as it should.

And at the top, there is nowhere to go but back down. Ups and downs of life are normal, and they are to be expected, but have you considered the great value of the rhythm of life? An unchanging comfortable life can become disorienting, and it is the comfortable life that slips by without warning. Too much comfort can produce risk aversion. Handcuffed to comfort, we lose the fight due to apathy; we just don't show up.

Comfort and stability are the enemies of growth. Beauty and wildness are outside the confines of comfort and predictability.

*"A ship in harbor is safe,
but that is not what ships are built for.
A ship in port is safe,
but that is not what ships are built for."*
- U.S. Navy Rear Admiral Grace Murray Hopper

If you want to build a ship, don't drum up the men and women to gather wood, divide the work, and give orders. Instead, teach them to yearn for the vast and endless sea."
-Antoine de Saint-Exupéry

Discomfort is not the point, but discomfort is necessary in discovering the point. Discomfort pushes you to try new methods and to experiment with new techniques. Comfort invites us to numb ourselves at the hearth. Do not fear discomfort, nor seek it. Pay no attention to comfort or discomfort. Pain is an indicator, do not ignore it, but don't concentrate on it either.

Think back to the pivotal moments in your life, the watershed times where for once you recognize you are making progress... can you identify the discomfort that preceded this event?

When was the last time that you allowed yourself to enter that same type of unknown? Maybe today is the day?

CONCEPT 029
/// Chaos Is Necessary, Irrationality Is A Rational Approach ///

Art correlates with discomfort.

Art makes the strange familiar, and the familiar strange.

Artists are called to enter into the chaos to create art. Funny enough, a good artist also brings chaos to the order.

To encounter chaos as a positive element, the artist has to have a loose grip on what most folks consider rationality. Art goes against the pragmatic grain; art forces us to relinquish pragmatism. "You are constantly thinking differently from what I am used to" is a coveted complement.

Culture places value on predictability, constantly calling you to become boring and normal.

Artists suffocate in predictability and are energized by the possibility of finding inspiration in the most unexpected places. Rational thinking is too constraining, disorienting artists in the attempt to learn the language of mystery.

Rational thought narrows the artist's focus, seeing the world through realist eyes. Imagination requires an escape from the cold hard facts, into the weirdness of imagination…

Art is not limited to the front door of rationality, but sneaks in the garage door and stretches the rational mind.

CONCEPT 030
/// Imagine No Resistance ///

Most of us are familiar with the phrase, "writer's block." Writer's block is approaching an imaginary brick wall in your mind that prevents further art and insisting on making the imaginary wall real. A temporary setback becomes a new way of life. The longer writer's block is allowed to prosper, the more writer's block you will have. Writer's block is the dog with his teeth firmly latched on to his own tail, unwilling to concede whilst yelping in pain.

Writer's block is the exhaustion of imagination against the reality of a deadline.

Resistance is common among creatives. Resistance can emanate from the isolation that you experience. Resistance is a real threat to a creative's forward progress. The paralysis of insecurity or confusion can render an artist unsure on how to proceed. Artistic resistance is similar to the "wall" that marathon runner speaks of.

Resistance is best addressed with a skilled coach and creative friends. Don't try to wrestle resistance, nor stare it down, you will only give your energy.

Be aware that resistance is coming. Resistance is always fighting for your attention and will cheat to win.

Respect resistance like you respect a rattlesnake, and avoid it rather than fight it.

Do not willingly submit to the slavery of paralysis.

Refresh your being, be kind to your soul, garden your creativity, and be patient.

CONCEPT 031
/// Home Is Not Where The heART Is ///

Home is a refuge when you are beaten down after a long day. Come home and unwind and sit naked on the couch as you eat a hot pocket and laugh at re-runs of Friends. Say what you will, do what you will, and home is still home, a place that withstands the worst of boorish behavior, and flat out wrong thinking – with acceptance an ocean wide. The entire world may spin out of control, yet stepping through the door the swirling stops, and at least here there is sanity, predictability, comfort, and for some of us an oversize pink Snuggie, the Blanket with Sleeves ... Home is the place that is most familiar to us.

If I were designing the universe, I'd have made rest and comfort the way to excel... want to be an Olympic Athlete; put your time in on the couch binge watching *This Is Us*.

When you get too comfortable with your art, you get lazy, and as a result, you start producing lazy art. Lazy art is the "help yourself to anything in the fridge, but get it yourself, feel at home" version of hosting.

Acceptance, sure, but the best of romantic diners take more effort than that. Sure, the "help yourself to anything" is great because it provides a family atmosphere that is inviting, vulnerable and intimate. Heck, feel free to fart out loud. Yet, on the other hand, some of the worst meals that we have ever eaten are from our own kitchen.

Grazing from the open fridge door is a desperate way to eat. Don't produce art that comes from the familiarity of your own kitchen and the resources that you have in your pantry. A sharp criticism of a narcissistic thinker is, "He eats his own cooking."

Push yourself to constantly impress yourself and the people that live with you (closest friends, etc.)

Those timid souls who never leave home, never really see or appreciate home. Like the old country and western song says, "How can we miss you if you won't go away?"

Get outside the box. Mom and apple pie will be there when you get back.

Habits and familiarity aside, live in confidence that familiar is available. Stay just lost enough, just strange enough, just far enough that it's not always clear how to return home. And for love of all that is sacred, please leave the room to fart.

CONCEPT 032
/// Self-Doubt 101 ///

Do you look in the mirror and love who you see, or do you have to improve the image before satisfaction?

Can you love and accept the reflected image with dried drool and a side of snot, or does the freshly-scrubbed-self get all the mirror love?

Humanity in the 21st century is about editing yourself, fixing yourself, making yourself presentable, consumable, looking as great as can be front of a never-satisfied public. Social media, anyone? We have to know the answers, we have to look like we have it all together. We have lost the art form of asking good questions.

We have a profound loss of shared curiosity, which has died at the hands of fear and narcissism.

I feel an irresistible pull to underdogs who produce conflict and turmoil art. Messy art. Open-ended question art. Not sure of the answer art. Not preachy art.

Turmoil artists have the courage to engage the spiritual narrative that things are broken, and that things are not as we hoped or intended. These artists are not scared of things that are broken.

Artists ready to admit ignorance and confusion produce the art that I trust the most. They create honest art revealing the human condition.

Love the doubting side of yourself, and for the love of Pete, quit trying to drown the poor chap.

Allow yourself the attractive quality of not knowing for sure.

On the other hand, know-it-all folks aren't constantly bombarded with all that social pressure like love and acceptance. Honest confusion, holding an unanswerable question for all to see, produces trust.

There's an old engineering axiom, "The more I learn, the less I know." As we learn more, we become more aware of all there is to know, and learning is a means to reveal to ourselves our own ignorance.

Embrace learning; it'll make you less sure, and more open to possibilities.

Art is birthed in the realm of possibilities, and dies in the realm of cocked-sure.

CONCEPT 033
/// What Does Freedom Feel Like? ///

Ever wonder where freedom is born? Ever marvel that the kids who live unguided and unsupervised lives grow into ridged conformist adults, and kids who grow up in nurturing homes, who can explore assisted within boundaries grow up to be open and free? The secret sauce of freedom is love.

Fear silences art, and religious fear is the worst.

Sadly, in the church, most of our freedom tends to be bookmarked by "What the Bible says" which is a smoke screen for "what I interpret the Bible to say."

The Bible is a window through which we see the life of Jesus, we see all that leads up to Jesus, and then we see Jesus. The entire book is about Jesus, and everything in it points to Jesus. Elevating the Bible to personhood in the Trinity is a really weird and idolatrous place.

May your constraints as an artist be love. Not necessarily the warm fuzzy kind of teenage puppy love. Sometimes love is the act of painting the ugly truth. But let love be your guide in art.

Scripture says, "fear is evidence of imperfect love," and I have witnessed this imperfect love repetitively.

Prophetic artists are desperately needed in the church today. Do not let the power of religious fear inhibit your art. Remember, Jesus was criticized because of his love for folks the religious leaders despised.

Produce prophetic art, and brace yourself for a tsunami of shit.

Criticism is part of the game, and when people invest energy into disagreeing, you can be sure you have their attention; therefore, you can be sure your art is working.

Do not put any weight on a hominem criticism. If they attack you, stand aside and let your art continue to do what it is surely doing.

Let the art help you with constraints. Let the constraints be in terms of creativity, not of moralism. Let love open the way, and resist the foreclosing of fear.

CONCEPT 034
/// Hatred And All Things Evil ///

Make art about what you're embracing, not what you're avoiding.

Make art about love, not hate.

I tend to find myself creating out of a desire to "make a statement" or "to prove someone else wrong." Where you focus, you give your energy. Don't energize hate.

Artists seek to unify communities and people. Musicians are sure their art is effective when people are dancing together. Art elevates the common good.

Don't require that your art meet your needs.

Create out of love.

Create out of a desire to bring people and ideas together, rather than to prove a point.

Points will be made and lost, but art lasts longer. Humanity is lonely. Humanity needs hope. We are longing for hope. In fact, we spend billions of dollars a year for anything that brings us together.

Let your art be the meeting-spot of lonely folks, create a shared moment for people to smile and connect.

Only paint for love, even if you have to paint love where there is none. There has been loving art made of Auschwitz.

Hatred will rot your soul if you stare at it long enough to create a portrait.

CONCEPT 035
/// Profit vs. Prophet ///

There is little profit in being a prophet.

Consider the Prophets found in the Old Testament of the Bible. If we define art as 'what one does to change the world,' they were amongst the greatest artists that have ever set foot upon the earth.

Prophets were the "voice of God" to the humans and the "representative voice of humans" to God. Often outcasts, they were misunderstood and considered irrational. Prophets created artistic content that is still discussed 6 thousand years later! The prophets were dealing with an artist's contemporaneous issues, but in doing so, they were dealing with aspects of the human condition. What prophets were about 6000 years ago is still relevant because while the problems have changed, humanity still has some consistent characteristics.

Art becomes timeless when the artist's contemporaneous challenge is grounded in the timeless human condition.

May the pull to profit never compete with the pull to prophet. Mass-appeal may not be a valid affirmation of art. Profits and prophets are enemies in nearly almost every area of life because of the inherent self-focus of profit. Occasionally, a prophet will create a piece that results in profit, but profit is never the motive.

The greatest prophet of all time is Jesus, and he was crucified for his trouble. Though his prophetic voice was able to change the world, it did not come with a beautiful income or retirement plan. In fact, it left him in isolation, with physical pain, emotional torment, etc.

However, this is the price that prophets will pay because they believe that they have discovered a truth that the world needs to be made aware of.

Make art that the world needs to be made aware of.

Jesus was nailed to a freaking tree. Don't assume your lot will be better. Just keep producing.

If your art serves primarily as a way to make money, just get a job and spare us. I have heard there's an opening in the band Nickleback. Don't spread your neediness in your art; it's bad enough on your Tinder profile. How you support yourself and how you change the world can come from different places. The demand that your art makes enough to support you is a demand for affirmation.

Your art is needed, the world is short of hope, but your neediness is a bore. Offer art, not need.

CONCEPT 036
/// Incoherence Is Not A Virtue ///

Art bears beauty of your identity.

There is a difference between mystery and incoherence; think the difference between freeform jazz and static on an AM radio.

Artful jazz requires us to ponder, to wonder, and to speculate. Static on the radio, or insincere art, leaves us scratching our heads and hoping we are not missing something.

Respect your audience with tension, with mystery, with art that makes room for others to participate.

There are 26 characters in our alphabet, and every thought in every library in America, and many of the thoughts on the Internet are expressed as combinations of 26 letters.

We make written art with a limited number of characters, and to be honest, I don't think that our written art would improve if we added twenty new letters to our alphabet. A book of scrambled letters might be useful to make some sort of visual art, but written art requires at least some sentence structure.

It can seem cool to make a word salad, to babble incoherently, to make incoherent art… but audiences don't embrace incoherence; they embrace mystery.

CONCEPT 037
/// Do Not Resign Too Quickly ///

I once watched a person trying to jack up a car, but they were completely unaware how the jack worked. It was painful to watch them struggle, and I was unable to intervene.

Ineptitude crossed with ignorance breeds hopelessness.

Hopelessness breeds a kind of soul death that also kills art in the cradle.

Artists are willing to risk ridicule and being misunderstood. Artists are brave enough to feel the empathy. Artists were often the first ones on the frontlines in Biblical battles... Coincidence? I think not. They are warriors.

Art has often kept the spark of hope of redemptive purpose alive in me.

We are not defined by our situation, unless we choose to be. Difficulty doesn't last forever, but a bad attitude can. Wonder imagines beauty, then draws its likeness.

Sometimes art emanates beautiful and the serene, even if it is chaos and injustice that fuel the artist's heart and soul.

Let yourself create art with the innocence of a child, but with the tools of an adult.

CONCEPT 038
/// Ahoy There ///

Ever experience someone in authority who is domineering, demanding, and graceless?

Chances are they are projecting their own anxieties onto whomever they have power over.

The captains of cruise ships have incredible authority. A single human controls a floating city that is 1200 feet long and housing 7,000 people.

Authority is what keeps him in charge. Temperament is why his staff trusts him.

With the same tempered authority, the artist captains the work; confidently free from anxieties and insecurities.

Like a sea captain, have you considered that your art should trust YOU?

No one can stop you from beating your art into submission.

Abused art is easily recognizable, under clichés and formalities. This art makes excuses for you, claiming *merely a flesh wound.*

Make art, not war… not even war with yourself.

CONCEPT 039
/// Addiction Is Overrated ///

Artists lend their identity to art; they don't receive their identity from art... in the same way driving isn't about being a driver.

Attempting to suck your identity out of your art is a form of addiction. In the way that every waitperson in LA is an actor, don't make your art be your identity's beast of burden.

Self-focus takes the focus from your art. Be inquisitive, be open, be light, don't be a boor.

Take art, but not too seriously. Take yourself, but far less seriously. Allow the planets to resume their orbits around the sun.

Let your art be a free-range-chicken, not stuffed in a cage forced to produce.

You and your art are friends, but for the love of Neptune, quit being so clingy. Your art won't leave you if you date someone else for the night. Have you ever considered your art might need a break from YOU? Confidently leave, knowing that your relationship to your art can withstand a night out... maybe even a sabbatical.

Don't use your art as an excuse to isolate; put some spice, some romance, some awakened desire back into your relationship to art.

Buy a thong.

Get jiggy with it.

It will still respect you in the morning.

Be yourself... separate from your art long enough to respect it and give it some space.

CONCEPT 040
/// Love Yourself, But Do Not Gloat ///

Every artist is allowed a self-portrait... but branch out a little. If all you need stares back at you from your bathroom mirror, trust me, your world has gotten too small. Art is a better window than a mirror.

Leave art fingerprints everywhere, and resist the urge to sign every work. Create for love and for wonder.

Be generous with your art.

Resist the urge to doctor and edit life and conform to some ideal; be known as you are today.

Scrolling through Instagram, it's amazing to see how staged and fake the offerings can be. Fake is so easily recognizable. Duck lips and filters and things perfectly staged on tables to appear organized and pleasing to the eye. Truth wins; let art showcase truth.

Continue breathing, be encouraged to keep fighting for your art. Bob Carlisle in his song "We Fall Down" has a brilliant line that states "the saints are just the sinners who fall down... and get up." Sanctify your art by getting back up after you feel like you cannot handle another blow.

Fight to leave a mark of beauty in this world.

The weak will give up easily. Respected art is appreciated after an artist has wounds to show.

Keep fighting to remain an image bearer of all of humanity in this moment.

Live fully in this moment.

Give us a glimpse of Eden in every piece that you create.

Be an artist of the particular that reveals the universal; open your art for all of humanity to find a place.

For 20+ years, I have loved the lyrics of the Delirious song "When All Around Has Fallen." In fact, on many occasions, this song has given me the power to get back up after taking what I consider to be the final blow. I have included them here:

> When all around has fallen
> your castle has been burned
> You used to be a king here
> now no one knows your name
> You live your life for honor
> defender of the faith
> But you've been crushed to pieces
> and no one knows your pain

Come, come lay your weary head be still my friend
Come, rise I'll place my sword upon your shoulder
Come, rise with me

When tomorrow has been stolen
and you can't lift your head
And summer feels like winter
your heart is full of stone
Though all your hopes have fallen
and your skin is now your only armor
Wear your scars like medals
defender of the faith

ABOUT THE AUTHORS

/// Heath Hollensbe ///
is more sinner than saint. He spent a majority of his career working in the music business and left it all a few years ago and moved to the Pacific Northwest where he works with the development of artists and creatives. He is the founder of the Elysian Society (ElysianSociety.com), which is an organization that hosts retreats and experiments for creatives. Heath is a massive fan of soccer and peaty Scotch Whisky. He is married to Kathleen, and they have 4 children (London, Rowen, Easton and Reagan). He and his family live in Fircrest, WA.

/// Vernon Hyndman ///
is a follower of Jesus, husband to Shelley since the 1980's, father to Zachary, Lauren, Kaitlin and Elijah. The offering of his life comes not from the career in bioengineering, nor the entrepreneurial years, nor pastoring to the broken and those who are not yet aware of their brokenness… but from a life of transforming brokenness held together by the baling wire of grace. Vern is beloved of Jesus, loved by others, and is committed to generosity of love and grace and peace. Vernon and his family live in Boiling Springs, PA.

www.ingramcontent.com/pod-product-compliance
Lightning Source LLC
Chambersburg PA
CBHW071105240526
45469CB00006BD/2336